SILENT CRIES

THE VIOLATED SPEAK

SILENT CRIES

THE VIOLATED SPEAK

CATHERINE MAGODO-MUTUKWA

Pen Featherz Media

An Imprint of TatendaCharlesMunyuki Publishing

SILENT CRIES: The Violated Speak

First published in Zimbabwe in 2015
Pen Featherz Media,
an imprint of Tatenda Charles Munyuki Publishing

ISBN   978 0 7974 6586 2

Typeset, printed and bound by Pen Featherz Media, Harare, Zimbabwe.
penfeatherzmedia@gmail.com

facebook.com/tcmpublishingzim

ACKNOWLEDGEMENTS

This book is in Partnership with SHAMWARI YEMWANASIKANA, a community based non-profit making, non-governmental organization which was formed with the aim of emancipating the girl-child from all forms of abuse.

I would like to thank the Director of Shamwari YeMwanasikana, Ekenia T. Chifamba and her team for making it possible for me to write and share these stories.
I would also like to thank Nompilo Maraire-Masikati for her assistance in compiling the stories as they came through.

And mostly, the individuals from which these true stories were derived from. I couldn't have done it without their stories.

Thank You All...

CATHY

There is no Justification to Abuse,
Neither Emotional nor Physical, Never in a
World we call ourselves
Civilized Human Beings!

Tatenda Charles Munyuki

INTRODUCTION

I was raised to believe that it takes a whole village, well in this case, a whole community to raise a child. It baffles me to learn that amidst our sometimes warm and all-seemingly loving homes, horrendous acts of crimes exist. In many instances, they are unreported and when they are finally prosecuted, the sentence handed down is usually a far cry from the pain endured by the victim.

For most of us, we fume and demand justice to the end product of a crime committed which is the right thing to do, but we forget about the times we stand by and watch a little boy or girl defenseless, helpless succumbing to ill-treatment and violation against their fragile bodies. We stand on the sidelines, too bothered to intervene but, *"how wrong we would be to stop helping anyone because we can't help everyone."*

In the world that we live in today, many have become heartless and cold. *Could we attribute all this to the social or economic circumstances? Could it be the regression of morals?*

Either way, there's absolutely nothing that can justify the stories of the young girls I'm going to share with you. Having partnered with *Shamwari YeMwanasikana (SYS)*, I have read and listened to heartbreaking accounts.

Getting their stories exposed into the societies might just help curb the violence against children in many ways and form.

Please note, names have been changed to respect and protect the victims.

2015   Catherine Magodo-Mutukwa

CHIPO AND CHIDO

I believe a father is an epitome of love, security, protection and honor. To a girl-child, he is the first male relationship she will ever encounter and thus she establishes her trust in him. It is a very sad situation when a father chooses to betray this trust just because he can as a calculating adult with an unruly behavior.

Chipo was only thirteen years old, barely a mature teen. Her father forced himself on her and threatened to kill her afterwards. He also went on to threaten her, if she ever told anyone about it. This happened on several occasions until she fell pregnant. He used lame excuses to pacify her, telling her that, this was the only way to prepare her for her grade seven exams and so it went on unnoticed for a long time.

Adding salt to injury, he cast his eyes on the younger sister Chido when she turned fourteen. Just as before, he sexually assaulted her and this time his excuse for doing so was, all the other girls in the village had gone through the same process with their fathers and that the intercourse would work as a lucky charm. Eventually, she too fell pregnant.

By the time the matter was reported, after their mother finally discovered what had been going on in her house, nothing much could be done. The father was arrested, tried and released in a short space of time to everyone's dismay. His defense was so outrageous and ridiculous as he claimed that his wife and daughters had conspired to have him arrested for sexual abuse that never happened just because his wife wanted to get back at him after asking for a divorce. Furthermore, the court pointed out that the girls did not provide enough evidence for prosecution, therefore their father had to be released.

A major blow to the girls, who will never see the face of justice to their ordeal at the hands of their father. One's heart bleeds, especially when obvious cruel men roam the streets free and unscathed, gloating over their invincibility while we watch on hopelessly. To the girls, the system that was supposed to come to their aid failed them. As they begin their journey, they are permanently marked with scars of a father who betrayed them.

Today we find the two girls staying with their mother, who helps raise the two inbred babies and looks after them while they go to school.

Shamwari YeMwanasikana also intervened and helps with baby clothes and provides counselling. Chipo hopes to become a nurse one day, perhaps her own way of helping others in the process of healing, while Chido dreams of becoming a bus driver.

VIMBAI

As many resort to different beliefs, many have turned to <u>muti</u> for a quick fix to their forever mounting problems. Whether for financial gain or healing purposes, often, in the centermost of such practices, you find the children being subjected to all sorts of heinous acts to the point of death.

Vimbai, in this story, is a six year old girl who was repeatedly raped by her father.

Barely surviving in abject poverty, their situation seemed helpless. It was most peoples' assumption that due to this condition, her father might have used her as *muti* to revive the family fortune or to bring one into existence. Her own mother knew of the incestuous relationship between father and daughter, but to everyone's surprise, no one understood why she couldn't fathom the severity and indecency of the manifestation.

Perhaps, just maybe, her husband may have threatened her so much so, if she ever said or did anything at all, he would inflict some form of danger or could it be, she might have been under his evil spell as well, hence everyone feared him. None-the-less, a six year old was being continually abused by her own family and it even got worse for this little girl when members of the society started taking advantage of the situation by raping her also.

It wasn't until Shamwari YeMwanasikana intervened that help for this little girl finally came. A community member alerted the organization after one of their massive campaigns and the child was rescued. Medical reports reviewed that, her pelvic bones had been fractured due to forceful entry and a police report was subsequently made and the perpetrator apprehended. Vimbai was put into a safe house where she is currently recuperating.

Shortly after the arrest was made, the case was heard in court, but to everyone's dismay and astonishment, today the man walks free, free to prey on other equally innocent girls. One has to wonder whether they will ever be justice for the young victims of brutal rapes.

Vimbai needs counseling in order to cope with her traumatic experience. As for the mother, one can only speculate on how she can ever live with herself.

Can we credit her actions to ignorance or lack of it? Having gone through such an ordeal, Vimbai is not deterred from pursuing her dream, which is music. She says it soothes her and hopes one day she will be able to sing and make something out of herself. Recently, a well-wisher came forward and pledged to pay for Vimbai's schooling so that she can attend school and possibly live a normal life for any girl her age.

TAMBUDZAI

As the HIV/AIDS pandemic continues to wreak havoc across the country and beyond, its deplorable that many children are orphaned resulting in displacement from their familiar surroundings, relocating with relatives who would have taken them in. Adjusting and settling down becomes the order of the day, but while all this is going on, some of the relatives who take on this crucial role of being guardians really play their part of providing and protecting very well while others have ulterior motives. A lot of children taken in by relatives have fallen prey to abusive situations, but the worst being that of violation against their little bodies.

*T*ambudzai was orphaned at a very young age and her aunt took her in. The aunt's family embraced her, after the sudden loss of both parents. She blossomed at first, but as time passed, she began deflating in enthusiasm and vigor. Reaching the age of puberty did not come with confusing hormonal changes only, it also brought along challenging situations where her aunt's husband, a father figure, started making suggestive moves on her. Her aunt was unaware of her reprobate husband's deviousness. Despite his oath to protect Tambudzai, he defiled her and she was never the same again.

After her rape, Tambudzai felt so ashamed that she couldn't even tell her aunt, fearing that her calamity would ultimately disrupt the family unit and bring shame and dishonor. Instead of facing her aunt, she chose to run away.

Usually, victims of rape are made to feel as if it's their fault that it happened to them, yet it's not. As for Tambu, she cried silently and opted for a life in the streets.

In the streets, as a runaway, she met a supposedly *good Samaritan*, a lady who took her in and instinctively took on the role of providing for her. Unbeknown to Tambu, she was living on borrowed time which she would later repay in kind. She had naively been conscripted into prostitution where she was forced to sleep with countless men. In her eyes, her very life became as worthless as her own body for a small change, but hefty price. She soon discovered, she was infected with same malady that took away her parents.

This sudden realization transformed her into a bitter and angry person. Tambu was furious at the world that never gave her a chance at happiness.

Only seventeen years old, she is a permanent resident of the streets of a certain city in the country refusing assistance. Perhaps in her mind she believes, *'it's a little too late.'* She also states that, the only thing she wants is death, as she awaits her fate unfazed.

This is however, a very prevalent anomaly as survivors try to deal with their experiences in different ways. Experts reveal that, it is much worse for a victim who has been raped by a relative or an acquaintance as trust there-forth becomes almost non-existent. Having been exposed to human fiendishness, Tambu displays feelings of numbness, anger, depression and therefore distances herself from anything that reminds her of love, the same love and compassion which was used to betray her.

Shamwari YeMwanasikana assists her with clothes and counseling whenever they get the chance.

RUDO

Young love ...new, exciting and full of butterflies, if it's the right time with right person. Despite all the advice and warnings, young girls still choose to involve themselves in relationships too complicated for their own age which quickly become burdensome to their inexperienced selves. However, there are certain men who actually prey on these virtuous girls, robbing them of their innocence. Young girls should note that older men are full of words, no action. They tell you what you want to hear until they lure you to a place of no return.

Rudo was just fourteen years and involved with a man whom she thought was younger and understanding. I'm sure he used every trick in the book to make sure he put her in a position where she could trust him. He came by her place one evening and asked her to accompany him to the shops. On their way there, he mentioned to her that he had forgotten his wallet at home, so they would have to go past his place in order for him to collect his wallet.

It was a plan well-orchestrated and in motion. As soon as they entered the house, the man's uncle excused himself and exited the door living Rudo and the man all alone in that house. She must have felt frightened, especially when this man started touching her inappropriately.

He must have been too strong for her because he managed to get her trousers off and proceeded to rape her. She must have begged him to stop, even screamed, but no one came to her aid in that house under the disguise of the night.

In spite of her ordeal, she somehow managed to get home where she told her mother of the attack. They hastily reported him to the police and investigations showed that this man was not a minor like he had initially stated to Rudo. In fact, he was an adult and so he would face his day in court, charged with statutory rape.

The hairs at the back of my head immediately rise at the knowledge of such an occurrence, wondering how many more girls he might have done this to, girls who did not come forward in fear of being labeled *'the guilty one'*, going to a man's house and regrettably ending up in the same predicament. Society is quick to judge, but there's never any justification for any man to do as he pleases with a woman's body without her consent just because he can.

As many of these girls recount their experiences one by one, one just can't stop, but feel the deep sense of loss of their chastity, the betrayal of the entrusted. It's something that once lost cannot be regained. To go through such encounters and live unscathed is an understatement.

They say time heals wounds of the past, but for many, the future will be a constant reminder of the past if most of us don't take a stand and fight for children's rights, particularly the girl-child. By empowering the girl-child with appropriate knowledge and education, we are arming her with the best defense for any manipulation at any given time. We are preparing her to be a better parent who will always be on the lookout for her own children and their future.

It begins at home, in our houses. Children don't learn from what they are told, but what is done in front of them. We would also be preparing her to be a better individual who will contribute positively to any society.

LAINA

I'm appalled at the extent at which some of these men go to take advantage of innocent girls. They pretend to be all so understanding, selfless and commendable, yet inside their evil heads, they are busy scheming no empathy for those grieving the loss of another. To the recently orphaned, it is a second chance at life without strife and too often this act of kindness turns back on them.

Laina, like Tambudzai, was also orphaned at a young age. Her uncle, father's brother, took her in and proceeded to take on the role of a father. A few years later, her uncle lured her to a construction site where he sexually assaulted her and the encounter resulted in pregnancy. Realizing the gravity of the situation if it ever came out, he forced her to illegally abort the pregnancy.

She said, she was taken to a place where they induced her leading to the birth of the child prematurely. She heard the baby cry, but she never held it, neither did she see or ever discover her baby's sex.

All she remembers is that they put the baby in a sack and the sack was thrown away somewhere and that was the last time she ever heard of it.

This inhumane act triggered a set of emotions in her which finally pushed her to come forward and report the matter to the police.

The uncle was eventually apprehended. Although his arrest won't bring back the child, at least justice was done by taking away freedom from this man who doesn't deserve to saunter the streets.

Shamwari YeMwanasika helps Laina with counselling, with advice on how to start income generating projects so that she establishes herself so as to be independent.

She now stays with an aunt in the Eastern Highlands.

Going through her story saddened as much as it sickened me, to imagine a grown man being sexually aroused by a minor, a dependent and be gratified is beyond sane.

It's mortifying to learn that, there are still people who harbor such sick people in the confines of their homes just for the sake of protecting a family's name.

They would rather have the child silenced than for the perpetrator to face the consequences of his actions.

Most incidences go unreported giving rise to a cycle of abuse, a cycle which needs to be broken in order to have a healthy, positive society.

KUNDAI

We can never understand sometimes, why bad things happen to good people, but there are those met with a fate unideal, who loathe daylight because they can't go on because of an experience at the hands of others.

Kundai was brutally raped by two men while going home one day. She kept it to herself. It wasn't until her legs began swelling preceded with unusual behavior that her father, concerned, thought to ask her. Kundai's father alerted the matter to Shamwari YeMwanasikana who got involved and pursued the matter until the two men were arrested. The case went to court, but to everyone's dismay, the two were only sentenced to community service. For Kundai, it made no difference at all. It seemed to her, her life henceforth would forever be tainted with the experience at the hands of these two monsters as she discovered she had contracted a STI and HIV. Despite all this horridness, she is however determined to go on with her life. SYS helps with school fees, counseling and they also encourage her to take her medicine.

TARIRO

Stability has always been recognized as the foundation for a grounded confident person. It is not always the case as the economic problems continue to strangle most peoples' pockets. Many are forced to move from one place to the other just to make ends meet and most orphaned children are not spared either. They are tossed from one house to the other just so it can be a shared burden but in the middle of all this tossing and sorting, many children fall victim to debatable individuals.

Tariro was thirteen years old when her parents passed. Soon she found herself being moved from one place to the other until she was taken in by her aunt's family. However, her aunt started physically abusing her as soon as she began staying with them.

She would get beaten and go on for days without food. She missed so many days of school that she was always repeating the same grade over and over.

A concerned member of the community reported the matter to the officials and Tariro was moved to her brother's house. While there, she began to settle and adjust, but in spite of this achievement, her older sister came and forcibly removed her from her brother's house and went with her.

Tariro's sister didn't do it for love, she wanted to exploit her for money. Arriving at her sister's came with mixed feelings as she found herself in the same predicament as before hence the sister was heavy handed with her. She started missing school again and there was talk of marrying her off or finding her a job just so she could be profitable. Tariro, who is supposed to have been in form two is still doing grade six because of all this instability.

Shamwari YeMwanasikana intervened and helped with counseling. It was discovered during one of the sessions that Tariro had been sexually abused by a cousin while staying with the aunt. She pointed out that she had told the aunt who had proceeded to silence her.

She lives in constant fear of being HIV positive. She also added that if found positive, she would report the cousin, but if not she would let it go and try to move on with her life.

Just like any other young girl, Tariro hopes to pursue and succeed in her studies so that she can further her education abroad. She wants to become an advocate for orphaned children and help make a difference in the lives of those in the same situation as her.

CHIEDZA AND NYARI

Abuse of any nature does have a negative impact on anybody at certain stage in one's life. As more and more children are subjected and exposed to situations beyond them, they develop coping mechanism just to numb the painful experiences whether physical or emotional. The damage done is usually difficult to mend, but with professional help of qualified therapists, we have witnessed many go on to become successful individuals who never forget where they came from, sharing their experiences just so it can help others. But for some, despite interventions, refuse to be helped at all. They choose rather a path with familiar abuse till they themselves succumb to the very thing they are trying to run away from... the abuse.

Chiedza and Nyari did not have a stable home after their parents divorced. They were always moved from one place to the other until their maternal grandmother took them in. Perhaps we can attribute their sudden change to their background as they became stubborn and rebellious refusing to listen to the voice of reason, that of their grandmother.

Although Shamwari YeMwanasikana was approached by the grandmother, efforts to counsel the girls proved futile as the two girls are reported to have run away from home leaving behind a distraught grandmother who fears being blamed if anything ever goes wrong with girls.

The two girls are currently looking for jobs as housemaids. Shamwari YeMwanasikana constantly keeps tabs on the two in an effort to convince them to return home and resume their studies.

WADZANAI

As we send off our children to school, we never think of it as a hunting ground for perverts. We anticipate safety and nurturing, while they acquire knowledge and grow in stature. Meanwhile, those of unscrupulous behavior expose their true colours, pouncing on unsuspecting little girls bribing them into selling off their innocence.

Wadzanai was sixteen years, studying for her Ordinary Level when one of the teachers convinced her to have an intimate relationship with him. The teacher would buy her gifts, perhaps to quieten her, making her feel special while he took advantage of her.

Wadzanai's mother became suspicious of the teacher-student relationship that had developed. One day, she followed her and caught them in the act. The mother reported the matter and investigations determined that this was not the first time the teacher was involved in something like this. It was unraveled that this teacher had been involved in affairs with young girls in the fourth form each year, knowing very well they wouldn't return the following year and his crudeness would therefore go undetected. The teacher was dismissed and the case went to court.

Shamwari YeMwanasikana came to Wadzanai's aid and offered her assistance and counseling. Wadzanai went on to do her Advanced Levels. She also joined the *National Girls Jury* supporting the rights of the girl-child. Although terrible, this experience helped her relate to many girls in the same situation as she now understands and appreciates a second chance in life, free of predatory characters.

TENDAI

The girl-child needs to be given a platform to voice out her fears, concerns and most importantly, be nurtured to become a confident, grounded woman.

Tendai lived with her paternal grandmother after her parents separated. She stayed with her for four years without any communication with her birth mother. Eventually, her mother organized for her to visit. As soon as she arrived, she started complaining of stomach pains. Probing the matter further, they discovered that her father's young brother had repeatedly raped her. They reported the uncle to the police and he was arrested. Tendai was just eleven years old.

It was ascertained that Tendai did not have a Birth Certificate during the process of the legal actions of the case which presented a problem. Shamwari YeMwanasikana intervened and helped her estimate her age, therefore obtaining a Birth Certificate for her. Tendai now stays with her grandmother who won custody and she is doing grade five.

In light of such cruelty, one cannot afford to listen and remain cross-handed. This appeals to me strongly knowing that it has become a common phenomenon in and around our gated neighborhoods. Silence is the price many of these girls pay, as they continue to suffer in silence because relatives and the community have painted a picture illustrating that, in the process, the girls would have asked for it or perhaps it must have been her fault to an extent, clearly diminishing the fighting spirit of others.

Somehow, it seems rallying behind these girls for justice is trivialized and tossed in the back of most ignorant minds as they go on with their daily lives, clueless of the effects rendered to the affected.

It is apparent from the stories that victimization of young girls has become as increasingly prevalent and disheartening.

In light of such acts, awareness has to be raised to educate the masses of transgressions brought on by abuse and their impact on the innocent souls.

Some of the girls do eventually learn to cope with their ordeal and go on with their lives, but for others adjusting doesn't come easy with many opting for suicide as thoughts and memories of the invasion continue to haunt them.

"It is not what we get, but who we become, what we contribute that gives meaning to our lives," and choosing to be part of an ongoing campaign to protect and educate the girl-child should be noted on everyone's agenda as this will make a big difference in generations to come and help break the cycle.

SHAMWARI YEMWANASIKANA

We envision a nation where girls are free and able to stand up for their rights with full support from the community and policies.

facebook.com/shamwariyemwanasikana
shamwariyemwanasikana@gmail.com
+263 717395754, +263 772607384
5 Chesterfield Road, Avonlea, Harare, Zimbabwe

black stars
The Beginning

Anthology consisting of a collection of poems from the talents of Catherine Magodo-Mutukwa, Lloyd Machacha, Tendai Mtukwa, Pearson Mbendera, Nicholas J Gorejena, Buhle Wendy Moyo and Simbarashe Chidakwa.

The anthology reveals the poets working on certain various themes and concerns, yet it exemplifies the diversity of their individual styles and identities.
It is the first of the black stars Anthology of Poems Series.

facebook.com/bstarzimanthology1

black stars

Sons and Daughters

Anthology consisting of a collection of poems from the talents of Catherine Magodo-Mutukwa, Lloyd Machacha, Tracy Dube, Sasha Melon, Edwin Msipa, Grace Furusa and Lesedi Evans Shumba.

The anthology focuses mainly on gender-based issues of both sexes, current, ancient and in transit.
It is the second of the black stars Anthology of Poems Series.

facebook.com/bstarzimanthology1

reflection

ANTHOLOGY OF POEMS

CATHERINE MAGODO MUTUKWA

Catherine Magodo-Mutukwa is a freelance writer and published author. Her exertion has been featured in Anthologies such as "We are one With or Without" 2014 published by Diaspora Publishers and "Black Stars: The Beginning" 2014 published by Pen Featherz Media (an imprint of Tatenda Charles Munyuki Publishing).

She exposes her feministic ideologies captivating simplistic, but intense writing style, which has been extended to her poems in REFLECTION An Anthology of Poems.

Cupid

Anthology of Poems

ANNAMARIA AYYAD, BRIAN MNKOSANA, EVELYN SCHRAUDER, BRITTA HOFFMAN, LLOYD MACHACHA, PAOLLA FLESSAK, TINA JOSEPH, PETER NJOVU, PHUMLA KHANYILE, MANG'ENI WYCLIFFE OBWOYA AND S.KOJO FRIMPONG in this Amazing Anthology from Poets around the World.

IT S ALL ABOUT LOVE

www.ingramcontent.com/pod-product-compliance
Lightning Source LLC
Chambersburg PA
CBHW020956180526

45163CB00006B/2387